lucid

ALSO BY DANIEL LOVE

Are You Dreaming?:
Exploring Lucid Dreams: A Comprehensive Guide

The Tao of Dreaming

DANIEL LOVE

Enchanted Loom Publishing

Published 2018 by Enchanted Loom Publishing

Special First Edition.

ISBN: 978-0-9574977-4-0

To dreamers and wanderers everywhere.

PREFACE

There are subtleties to the lucid realms. These unique states of mind at the fringe of human experience are, by their very nature, almost impossible to portray. For most of human history these strange and unutterable modes of being have been the domain of philosophers and mystics.

This work is a reflection of my own journey into these spheres, in the hope that those seeking to explore beyond the core experience of lucid dreaming will be inspired and prepared to do so.

As a rational voice in the field, I hope to bring some of the deeper mysteries of the mind to those who have yet to venture into this territory.

Lucidity is a remarkable phenomenon, and for even the most ardent rationalist its sheer peculiarity warrants a re-evaluation of one's relationship with the cosmos.

In my work as a lucid dream and consciousness researcher, one of the most common questions I'm asked is to describe my personal and philosophical relationship with lucidity. This book is an attempt to address this directly.

Rather than the now commonplace instructional works on lucidity, this book's goal is to approach the topic from a different angle, sitting somewhere between art and philosophy.

This is not a guidebook in the traditional sense. Instead, this is a collection of mind-seeds, ideas that I hope will take root in the unique soil of your psyche and grow according to your own private life-journey. Lucidity is, above all, a personal adventure. A guide can only point the way, you must forge your own path.

If you are a beginner looking for a "how to" book on lucid dreaming then I'd highly recommend picking up a copy of my previous book, "Are You Dreaming?", as "Lucid" acts as its philosophical companion and is best read afterwards. The two act to balance one another.

While I'm not fond of the popular myth of the dichotomy between the left and right brain, it is a useful metaphor for the relationship between these books. Seen through this lens, "Are You Dreaming?" can be considered a left-brain approach to lucidity, a step-by-step and logical take on the subject. "Lucid", on the other hand, represents a right-brain perspective, as it reflects a more intuitive and creative journey, exploring the more ineffable aspects of a lucid life. It is certainly vastly different in content and style from its sister.

Throughout this book the term lucidity will be used interchangeably, either to represent lucid dreaming (dreams in which one knows one is dreaming), or waking lucidity (those magical moments of clarity in which one feels fully present in the moment, aware of our place in a vast and mysterious cosmos). This choice is intentional.

My own journey into lucidity has made it abundantly clear that the two states are strongly interconnected. Indeed, the lucidity that occurs in dreams is something of a microcosm, a reflection of a deeper mode of thought and being.

From the perspective of an author, this book has been a fascinatingly challenging and personal project. Those familiar with my style will be aware that I extensively research and explore my topics. Often this requires a certain degree of wordiness. However, the core principle behind this book is that of lucid-minimalism. I have attempted to condense the most salient aspects of lucidity, in an attempt to capture its essence in the hope that you may be inspired to explore this practice in your own way.

Needless to say, for a man who enjoys meandering verbal journeys, it has been a fascinating experiment to rein in this natural tendency and focus on linguistic distillation. I even felt a degree of hesitancy in sharing this very personal side of the path, as the style, content, and approach required a distinct baring of the soul.

The well read among you will notice that I have drawn considerable stylistic inspiration from the writings of Laozi, author of the Tao Te Ching. Lucidity, as with the Tao, contains many inexpressible elements. Indeed, some may argue that they are both paths leading to the same destination. The keen-eyed will notice that "Lucid" shares the same 81 verse structure as the Tao Te Ching (minus this introduction). This is deliberate.

I also have been strongly influenced by the principles of Zen, Minimalism and the Haiku—the flavours of which clearly infuse this work.

Indeed, the idea of encapsulating wisdom into simplicity and art so it may flower in the minds of others seems ideally suited to the teaching of lucidity. It is, I believe, one of the most potent means of doing so.

As a lifelong lucid dreamer, I have become aware that, when taken seriously, lucidity is a lifestyle rather than just an unusual nocturnal goal. Much of its practices and skills embed themselves in one's daily psychology and impact one's philosophy; lucid dreaming quickly transforms into lucid living. It is this, the life of a lucid dreamer, which this book aims to enrich.

While the techniques and science of lucidity are incredibly useful, other literature has explored these ad nauseum. Therefore, it feels right to approach the topic from a new angle, something closer to philosophy or spirituality, without the usual accompanying metaphysical baggage.
The shadowy depths of the dreaming and waking mind operate in a creative, mythical and abstract fashion, a principle that ancient teachers, with their ample use of parable and metaphor, knew very well. Often the best strategy for achieving psychological change is to speak directly to the subconscious in its own language, that of art and poetry.

I suggest that the reader approach this book as a series of meditations. It is not designed to be read cover-to-cover. Instead, I'd recommend dipping in and out of its pages whenever you find a quiet moment. Then use each verse as a trigger to further explore its concept.

This book is designed as a lucidity technique in itself. It adopts the most potent means to induce lucid thinking, namely regularly immersing oneself in the concept. In short, carry this book with you and use it to inspire private contemplations.

The style of each verse varies dramatically, including straightforward practical advice, metaphorical parable, poetry, and everything in between. Each, I hope, acts as a distillation of a much larger idea—one that is best lived rather than described. I ask the reader to view this book as one would a gallery, as a place for inspiration.

With the principles of minimalism in mind, the aim was to fit each verse onto a single page. With a few exceptions, I have largely achieved this goal. In fact, this was also a fortunate side effect of one of the creative process behind the book. The experiment in question consisted of asking prominent characters from my own dreams to express what they believed should be included within these pages.

Due to the limitations of short-term memory, this resulted in a natural filter, limiting that which could be transferred between worlds. With this in mind, it is important for the reader to understand that much of what is included within comes from oneiric personalities and sources beyond my daily comprehension.

I am aware that the style of this book may be a surprising diversion from that which my readers are accustomed. However, I can assure you that the principles of reason and critical thought remain more firmly than ever at its foundations.

While the style may seem unusual to the modern reader, maybe even tickling the toes of pretentiousness at times, I believe that lucidity is a timeless aspect of the human journey, more important than the individual preferences of others or myself. Lucidity deserves a style that reflects its profound nature.

The 81st verse, "Unplug", is one of the few that deviates from the minimalistic approach. In fact, it was originally written independently. I've included it here as it encapsulates a few of the more pressing issues of our time. It also holds a certain personal significance as it marks the beginning of my own acceptance of the importance of lucid-minimalism—a concept which, throughout my life, I have found myself returning to again and again.

Do not be misled by the seeming simplicity of many of these verses, each has been carefully crafted in much the manner of a Zen koan. I believe that for those of you ready to explore the deeper levels of lucidity will, through your own travels, discover the messages buried within.

I hope that the ideas shared within this book are of value in your own remarkable explorations of what it means to be lucid in this vast and beautiful cosmos.

I must thank the community of lucid dreamers for allowing me the opportunity to embark upon such an unique project. It is only through their support that this work could come to life.

Special thanks goes to Nyx.

D.B.L.

SIMPLICITY

Through simplicity,
One distils meaning and truth.
Life becomes lighter.

STILLNESS

Stillness is a key to the lucid mind.

It is the foundation upon which awareness rests.

When one peels away the many layers of mind to confront one's core, one finds the still and darkened canvass of awareness.

Lucidity requires one to remain calm and patient, to avoid entanglement in the kaleidoscope of distractions.

Only when one can sit in this simple tranquillity, unshaken by the storms that pass, will dreams flood to fill in the void.

Do not force, do not will.

By embracing emptiness and accepting the blank canvas of the mind, one allows the inner artist to set upon painting the world of dreams.

Be as still as an artists model, awaiting the final brushstroke.

Only then can one explore the art.

FOCUS

Spend a little time each day exploring the varied elements of perception.

Become aware that each moment is an amalgam of sensory information.

Take time to live through a specific sensory point: experience the world as, perhaps, a hand, toe, ear, nose, or knee.

Invest your full awareness into its sensory world, learning to appreciate its unique experience.

Consider each sensory exploration a voice in the choir of perception.

Through this practice you will learn that focus is a tool, muscle and lens.

Build, refine, and sharpen your focus—it will serve you well.

DEDICATION

Lucidity is not a form of magic, nor a spiritual reward. One cannot wish it into existence.

It is only through careful cultivation that the flower of lucidity will grow.

Ignore those who would sell short-cuts or belittle the importance of discipline.

Lucidity requires one's full attention, critical faculties, energy, experimentation, and curiosity.

One does not embark upon a journey without preparation, nor complete it without investment.

VARIETY

Dreams are the honey of the mind, flavoured from the flowers of waking experience.

Choose a varied and sweetly scented bouquet.

TECHNIQUES

Lucidity cannot be forced.

Dreams are butterflies who visit when the conditions are correct.

To know them one must first see beyond the distractions of their many coloured flutterings.

To attract them, one must become still and observant.

To guide them, one must learn their nature.

Techniques are but nets and flowers, a useful starting point to initiate understanding.

Once realised, a dedicated dreamer becomes a gardener of the mind, cultivating the perfect environment.

The definitive technique is not a technique: it is a botanical garden.

EXPLORATION

We are explorers.

Our ancestors struggled through darkness and mystery, slowly igniting the torch of human knowledge.

Developing the skills of lucidity is a means by which to carry forward that torch.

Through logic, awareness, science, experimentation, imagination, philosophy, and a hunger for understanding, we carve our tracks into the future.

Every aspect of life offers a chance for exploration.
There is a world to be discovered in every happening.

Even the simplicity of a petal hides a universe of staggering complexity and knowledge.

Lucidity embodies the heart of art, science, exploration, and philosophy.

A lucid mind is an explorer's mind.

WILD

To fall into a dream from wakefulness, retaining critical awareness, is known as a Wake Initiated Lucid Dream.

There are many techniques for remaining aware during the transition.

One may count, imagine pulling oneself up by a rope, visualise exotic symbols, or use many other means.

The principle behind each remains the same.

Regardless of the variations in technique, all that is required is to carefully balance relaxation and continued reflective awareness.

Do not mistake technique for purpose.

Each mind is unique.

Experiment and discover your own tools for maintaining balance.

BALANCE

Imagination carries us into the world of dreams, but only with rational thinking do we become aware.

These are the two inseparable elements of a lucid dream.

A lucid life reflects this. It is the process of blending these two complementary aspects of self and recognising their inherent oneness.

On the stage of humanity, it seems that the inner conflict between imagination and reason plays out; magnified and transformed into religiosity and science.

When rationality lacks heart or momentum, it can be enhanced with art, stories and imagination.

When imagination becomes unhinged or senseless, our critical faculties can act as an anchor.

Strive for a bridge between these two worlds, a middle way, a corpus callosum.

REALITY

It is easy to get lost in the dream of life, to sleepwalk through existence.

Sometimes it seems that we only become aware of our fragile and astounding existence during moments of grave peril or intense emotion. They shock us into realising who and where we are.

So too with dreams: often lucidity arises when the mind serves a dish too intense to ignore.

By cultivating a more enduring astonishment at reality, a childlike wonder, we move towards a life in which each moment is lucid.

While life can be both beautiful and terrifying, a dream and a nightmare, with a little more awareness we become stronger, braver and better equipped to face reality.

The shadows lose their teeth and the world shines a little more brightly.

RIDDLE

01001001 01100110 00100000 01111001 01101111
01110101 00100000 01101000 01100001 01110110
01100101 00100000 01110100 01101000 01100101
00100000 01100011 01110101 01110010 01101001
01101111 01110011 01101001 01110100 01111001
00100000 01100001 01101110 01100100 00100000
01110100 01100101 01101110 01100001 01100011
01101001 01110100 01111001 00100000 01110100
01101111 00100000 01110011 01101111 01101100
01110110 01100101 00100000 01110100 01101000
01101001 01110011 00100000 01110010 01101001
01100100 01100100 01101100 01100101 00101100
00100000 01110100 01101000 01100101 01101110
00100000 01111001 01101111 01110101 01110010
00100000 01101101 01101001 01101110 01100100
00100000 01101001 01110011 00100000 01110111
01100101 01101100 01101100 00100000 01100101
01110001 01110101 01101001 01110000 01110000
01100101 01100100 00100000 01110100 01101111
00100000 01100101 01101101 01100010 01100001
01110010 01101011 00100000 01110101 01110000
01101111 01101110 00100000 01100001 00100000
01101100 01110101 01100011 01101001 01100100
00100000 01100101 01111000 01110000 01101100
01101111 01110010 01100001 01110100 01101001
01101111 01101110 00100000 01101111 01100110
00100000 01101100 01101001 01100110 01100101
00101110 00100000 00001101 00001010 00100000

PHANERON

The phaneron is the world as one experiences it.

It is the mental model of the cosmos as filtered by sensory input and contained by biological hardware.

The phaneron is the collective total of all that exists within the mind. It is a phantom realm, a unique nexus of perceived reality, memory, impulse, instinct, emotion, and creative imagination.

The lucid mind accepts that all experiences, be they dreams, hallucinations, or waking life, are lived entirely within the confines of the phaneron.

This realisation helps the lucid explorer to reshape her relationship with reality, to understand that her life is a creative interpretation.

When one fully comprehends this principle, the perceived barriers between the waking and dreaming worlds evaporate.

CONFORMITY

A lucid mind is not the product of conformity.

To become lucid within our dreams we must first cultivate a mind that is free to question everything.

Non-lucid dreams are the epitome of conformity, they are a blind acceptance of that which is presented: a world of face-value.

Conformity comes in many guises. It is not only the adherence to popular social convention or authority.

We must also question our most cherished beliefs, unpick the subtle patterns in our lives, even dissect those areas in which we consider ourselves unique and unusual.

Scepticism is one of the most powerful tools for carving a clear and lucid mind.

Confront the fear of asking taboo questions. Be brave and place truth before the need for acceptance.

DISRUPTION

While disruption can be perceived as negative, it is often a powerful solution to stagnation.

To achieve a lucid dream one can disrupt the natural cycles of sleep in order to inject awareness into unconscious stupor.

By observing and understanding the patterns of the sleeping mind, we discover periods in which dreaming is most prevalent. This is generally during the final hours of sleep but may vary depending on our unique nature.

Experiment with the disruption of the sleep cycle and learn from the results.

Equally, if your practices are not yielding rewards, do not be afraid to break patterns or explore new avenues.

Much as plough disrupts soil in order to give life to new seeds, in life, the introduction of a little disorder can often lead to new and unexpected outcomes.

EXPERIENCE

Imagine laying on your deathbed reviewing the events of your life.

Ask yourself: exactly how many of my material possessions would I miss?

Would you waste even a moment's time wishing to be reacquainted with a long forgotten ornament or favourite item of clothing?

Instead, consider which aspects of your life you'll truly cherish in those last moments.

Is it not more likely that it will be the smile of a loved one, laughter with friends, adventures, beautiful environments, soaring music, and exhilarating moments?

Experiences are the currency of the spirit.

They are the fabric from which a meaningful life is woven. Both our dreams and lives are built from them.

CONFLICT

Dreams often reflect inner conflicts and unresolved psychological issues.

Therefore, it is important to inject awareness into any troublesome, confusing or emotionally charged moments of wakefulness.

By allowing oneself to step back, observe, and reflect during the tumultuous emotional events of life, one forges a habit that will, in time, transfer into the world of dreams.

Simply and sincerely asking the question, "Is this a dream?" can be enough to initiate a calm and still space in which lucidity can flourish.

By inviting detached awareness into the storms of life, we increase our freedom and clarity in all modes of existence.

Lucidity dwells in the eye of the raging storm.

ATTENTION

We are neural forests.

Tend to the ideas you wish to flourish,
Prune those which you wish to maintain,
Ignore those which you wish to wither.

Ideas are born, live, and die in accordance with attention.

Repetition forms habit,
Habits become actions,
Actions forge life.

CRITICAL

Critical thinking is the primary tool for navigating our dreams and lives with lucidity.

Our critical faculties allow us to escape our instinctual and biological programming, breaking us free from blind reaction and emotional fog, offering us reflection and analysis in their place.

A lucid dream is a dream in which the scenario has been critically analysed and the correct conclusion, that it is all a dream, drawn according to all available evidence.

So too, a lucid life is one lived bravely questioning and investigating all that is presented.

Critical thinking is a candle that dispels the shadows of ignorance and allows us to navigate existence clearly.

MANTRA

A mantra is a simple tool utilizing repetition in order to strengthen focus, develop habit, and program neural pathways.

Language is the operating system for self-reflective awareness. It defines the border between the archaic and modern modes of thought.

It is language with which we consciously define and inspect ourselves and experiences.

A mantra is not some magical phrase or spell.
It is a carefully constructed linguistic tool designed to inject new programming into your psyche.

Mantras can be used as aids in defining and achieving any objective in life.

Experiment with the construction of your own unique mantras.

Use simple, powerful, focused, descriptive and memorable language.

CREATIVITY

If one wishes to enhance creativity in either the dreaming or waking state, one must loosen the reins of control.

Creativity flowers in chaos. It is the unbounded mind playing with infinite possibilities.

It is easy to mistake lucidity for control, but while lucidity lends awareness to influence, it does not necessitate it.

Freedom, exploration, and uncritical observation allow creativity to flourish.

Creativity cannot be compelled, one must simply set the stage, let go of expectation, and allow the mind to dance.

EXPECTATION

Expectation is the loom upon which dream control is woven. It is also a powerful tool for influencing one's perception and the outcome of events in waking reality.

The dreaming mind acts as an expectation feedback system, working with both overt conscious expectations, and the subtle assumptions that underpin one's psychological landscape.

In dreams, that which is expected comes to pass.

Understanding the exaggerated power of expectation within the dream world allows us to master its influence in life.

To become familiar with the feeling of actualised expectation, meditate by repeatedly flipping a coin and attempting to "will" its outcome. Pay attention to the difference in feeling between expected and unexpected outcomes.

Remember the sensation and explore its power to control the dreamscape and, in time, waking life.

NATURE

We live in a constructed world that almost entirely reflects the will, needs, and imagination of humanity.

In doing so we have sidelined nature, reducing it to little more than decoration, curiosity, or nuisance.

For many of us, our lives are spent isolated from the feral spirit of the universe. We exist in a polished hall of mirrors reflecting humanity's conceits, ambitions, flaws, and strengths.

It is important to remember that our minds have evolved to interact with nature, to unriddle her mysteries, to translate the language of the untamed.

The mind is a force of nature.

Taking time to regularly break free from the bubble of humanity, to explore nature face to face, can be a potent means by which to reorientate and reset one's perspective.

SILENCE

For sentience there is no true silence.
When one seeks silence, one discovers oneself.

JOURNEY

It is easy to become blinded by ambition.

A novice lucid dreamer can often live in a state of frustration, forever awaiting the next success and berating failure.

It is important to enjoy the journey of lucidity and avoid becoming obsessed with outcome.

Each non-lucid dream is a valuable lesson and an important experience in its own right.

We must accept and learn our limitations to appreciate the perfectly imperfect nature of consciousness.

We should push ourselves forward but avoid setting unrealistic expectations.

An archer who holds his bow too firmly will miss the target and quickly tire.

Be fluid and playful and enjoy all aspects of the journey.

MAGIC

Learning the skills of parlour magic can be a very useful practice for those seeking a deeper understanding of the mind.

Magicians are experts in exploiting the subtle quirks and shortcomings of human perception.

Even the most rudimentary understanding of the secrets behind their illusions will offer tangible examples of the limitations and processes behind one's experience of the world.

Magic instils a rare form of humility and aids in the development of a unique and healthy scepticism, one that dispels metaphysical credulousness.

SAFETY

There are no safe spaces in our universe.

Each of us is but one event away from disaster and oblivion.

No amount of wealth, status, power, security, beauty, health, friendship, youth, or wisdom can shield you.

Existence is both beautiful and terrifying.

Only when we can accept the universe on its own terms, unafraid of reality's fangs, can we live full and lucid lives, truly awake to the brief dream of existence.

AUTHORITY

The world is full of those who would claim authority over your journey.

Remember, you are a unique expression of the universe.

While others may offer guidance or useful field notes, you alone decide your path.

We all yearn for answers.
We long for a cosmic parent or spiritual saviour to untangle the riddle of existence.

But it is braver and wiser to accept that we are all adrift, all explorers, all searching.

Be wary of those who claim authority or sell comforting answers to the most ancient of questions. They too were born naked and lost.

COINCIDENCE

It is imperative for those wishing to increase dream lucidity to become mindful of coincidence—to use it as a trigger to question the nature of reality.

Dreams are forged through expectation and, therefore, are ripe with coincidental events.

The study of coincidence during waking life, including the the mathematical principles of chance, helps one to break the impulsive response of assigning metaphysical cause to events.

Become a connoisseur of coincidences. Observe their nature and study the science behind their appearance.

They are a doorway to deep and fascinating worlds of knowledge.

TRUTH

Truth is cold.
Truth has no stake in human desires.
Truth is lucidity.

Holding firmly to the truth is not easy. Our minds ache for comforting delusions and a reassurance of their own importance.

A journey into lucid living will uncover ugly, awkward, terrifying, and profound truths.
It will shake the foundations of your identity.

Truth is death, decay, shame, and horror.
Truth is life, beauty, pride, and passion.

But, a life without truth is a clouded illusion, a shadow of reality.

Strive for honesty even when the truth is hard. It is the only way to wake from the dream.

TIME

Now.

LOST

You and I are strangers lost in an ancient and mysterious cosmos.

For all of our bravado, we spin helplessly through infinity, adrift in an unfathomable riddle.

If there are truths, we will never know them all.
If there is more to life, we can only guess.

We are fragile creatures, infants stirring in a primeval womb.

Our shared existence is beyond explanation, we simply are.

We are lost, but in each other we can find comfort and kindness. We are fools, but together we will uncover fragments of understanding.

My words are a child's scrawl on the impenetrable wall of mystery: they state “I am”.

For all their simplicity, I hope they remind you that while you journey alone, you are not.

PARALLEL

Dreams are a parallel world, a second life, an alternative self.

While much of our dreamworld reflects the scenes and concerns of the material world, it is important to avoid mistaking them for carbon copies of the original.

As a lucid dreamer, it can be advantageous to think carefully when choosing one's material possessions. Consider both their waking use and potential dream application.

This can be particularly useful for those items that decorate your bedroom, as this is a common starting point often replicated in dreams.

For example, a large mirror could become a dream doorway, a figurine can become imbued with the spark of life, or a rug can transform into a magical flying carpet.

The possessions of a lucid dreamer can live secret parallel lives, shimmering with hidden magic.

MUSIC

Music is the cousin of dreams. Each is ineffable, transcendent, and brimming with emotion. Their relationship is complex and worthy of investigation.

In dreams we find all manner of tunes, from familiar modern songs to the half-remembered music of our youth.

In almost all cases, the sheer level of recall and reproduction is astounding, a fine example of the fascinating depth of human memory.

Equally, music can be used to influence our dreams and promote lucidity.

Falling into sleep while listening to music can shape one's dreams or act as an anchor upon which we fasten our awareness—a reminder to remain conscious as we drift into the oneirosphere.

Explore the power of music to enhance your dream adventures.

ESCAPISM

There once was a man who lived in mystery.

Having never taken the time to notice the wonders around him, he became quite entangled in the concerns of the mundane.

Becoming obsessed by the idea of something more, but blind to his surroundings, he took up the tools of his world and built a machine of wonders, a device that would allow him to live a second life.

After many years spent living in this new artificial world, he remained unsatisfied; for all of its shimmering delights, it was hollow.

Still hunting for more, he lay his head upon a simulated pillow and drifted into a synthetic dream.

Once again, many moons passed in this queer and magical dream but eventually it became apparent that this world was a mere reflection, equally as unsatisfactory.

Searching still, he took to hand a dream pen and decided upon writing a novel: he would live within its story.

As the pages turned, he played many characters, shifting

from one scene to the next, falling deeper and deeper, entangled within its prose.

He was lost under many layers, deep within a maze of illusions.

As time passed, and as the tale unfolded, he became old and forgetful.

Memories of the real world had long since blurred and faded.

He drifted from one page to the next, itching with ennui and fogged confusion.

Longing for simplicity and true adventure, he decided to transform himself into a single sentence, one final attempt to realise his deepest desire.

It read:

There once was a man who lived in mystery.

LITERATURE

There are many means for influencing dream content.

One of the most potent is the consumption of literature, especially works of fiction.

The tales and landscapes of the written word exert a profound influence on the dreamscape.

An engaging novel ignites the imagination and fine-tunes one's ability to visualise. Fiction injects unsolved mysteries into the mind.

One of the primary functions of dreaming is the examination and exploration of current preoccupations. An engaging tale offers a fantastic means of embedding riddles into the dreamworld.

Therefore, it is important to choose one's fiction carefully, in the knowledge that it will be revisited and expanded upon within dreams.

It is useful to experiment with this principle.
Remember, in dreams, you are what you read.

EMOTION

It is clear that dreams are abundant in emotion.

In sleep our passions soar. We experience deep loves, bitter hatred, joy, rage, the entire spectrum of human emotion.

We can use this tendency to increase lucidity within our dreams.

During waking hours, be mindful of emotional states and learn to use them as triggers for lucidity by questioning reality whenever they arise.

Equally, explore the nature of emotion. Ask yourself: if in dreams we can experience passions equal to their waking counterparts, do they differ in value?

Are emotions a response to events or are we the artists of our own emotional landscapes?

Should we search for love, happiness and pleasure externally or within?

SCENT

Scent has a long historical association with memory. An aroma can instantly transport the mind back to a moment in which it was previously experienced.

The structures of the brain offer a glimpse into the reasons behind this. The area of the brain responsible for the analysis of scent is closely connected to the amygdala and hippocampus, the areas responsible for memory.

For the lucid explorer, this represents a practical means of influencing dream content and the triggering of associations in waking life.

By carefully associating scents with certain people, places or emotions, we can then invoke their presence in the dreamworld by using the same perfume upon our pillow.

Equally, a handkerchief doused in a perfume one has previously associated with a pleasant emotion, can be used to calm and soothe an unpleasant waking experience.

MINIMALISM

Lucidity lends itself to minimalism.

Observe that the mind is the stage on which plays out the story of life.

See that it is the source of all experience.

Hunger for the material diminishes.

Learn that striving for material gratification is an eternal itch: with only temporary relief.

Loss can only exist when one invokes attachment.

In emptiness there is infinite potential.

PATIENCE

We live in a world of instant gratification. As our technology grows, we increasingly expect our whims to be swiftly satiated.

However, lucidity, be it in dreams or life, requires a glacial degree of patience.

As with any skill of value, one must be prepared to invest time and dedication into its development.

Remember, the mind is organic, and while our reflexes and processing skills are swift, our neural architecture evolves with steady consistency.

To remind oneself of the gentle pace of progress, it can be helpful to invest in a small houseplant to represent and reflect one's own development.

Observing and nurturing its slow and imperceptible growth will act as a constant reminder of the true rate of one's journey.

EQUILIBRIUM

It is common for those striving for a goal to invest unsustainable levels of energy.

Lucidity is a lifelong journey and so starting with a sprint will only serve to wear oneself out—risking exhaustion and disillusionment.

Pace yourself.

Passion should be tempered with prudence.

Strive for equilibrium in your practices.

EYES

The visual cortex is one of the largest systems in the human brain.

Indeed, our relationship with sight is deeply entwined with our experience of reality, often in subtle and unexpected ways.

For example, it is believed that the whites of the eyes, a feature lacking in most mammals, evolved due to our highly social nature and as a means to communicate the direction of our attention.

In the pursuit of lucidity, it is valuable to develop the skill of maintaining eye contact with others.

To do so, strive to become observant of the details in others' eyes, their elaborate patterns of colour, their movements during thought.

With this practice you shall develop a more commanding and empathic nature, deepen relationships, improve confidence, and increase lucidity during interactions.

These skills shall enhance your life and imbue your dreams with clarity.

MAP

A lucid explorer should become a cartographer of consciousness.

The recording of a detailed and honest journal, for both dreams and lived experiences, allows for the collection of an invaluable trove of unique personal knowledge.

To understand oneself, there is simply no better teacher, and no better book, than your own journal of adventures.

Consider your journal an ever-expanding map of the landscape of your soul.

In doing so, one embraces the principles of science and exploration, carefully recording the idiosyncrasies and geography of the psyche.

The journal is a magical mirror reflecting the evolution of the self. It is your most loyal guide and companion.

COMPANIONS

The journey towards lucidity is a solitary path.

However, it is important to maintain a level head and ample humility.

The human mind is prone to self-aggrandisement and circular proclivities.

To counter egotism, it is helpful to share your thoughts and experiences with others. Do so with a mind that is open and eager to accept criticism and confrontation.

Do not surround yourself with only sycophantic or like-minded individuals. Instead, choose companions with a broad spectrum of beliefs.

Allow yourself to be challenged and explore opposing ideas.

Be prepared to be wrong, as this will often be the case, and gracefully accept the opportunity to grow.

FEAR

Fear is natural and should not be avoided.

Our modern world, filled with its comforts and advances, is a luxury quite unlike the world of our ancestors. We evolved in a world of tooth and claw and we carry this legacy within us.

Fear is a natural response, an instinct no less vital than happiness or hunger. True fear is, fortunately, a rarity in our times, and in becoming so it has transformed.

In our relative safety, without a natural outlet for fear, it has distorted, becoming irrational and phobic.

We have grown to fear fear itself.

For most, true terror is most commonly only experienced in nightmares—as our minds strive to oil this primal system.

Consider fear an ancient ally. It is both a guide and a tool for growth. Face and embrace it and you will become stronger.

INNOVATION

When facing the challenges of lucidity, one must be prepared to innovate.

Exploration requires an inventive mind, one prepared to assess the inner-landscape, and devise novel solutions to unique problems.

A lucid mind is a pioneer of new frontiers, an adventurer into the unknown.

One must shake off the coddling of society and embrace one's own responsibility to unravel and solve whichever mysteries present themselves.

Others may offer guidance but this is a lone journey.

You alone will forge the path.

You alone invent your future.

PRODUCTS

There are a seemingly endless supply of products on offer to aid your journey.

Be they pills, machines, software, books, workshops, or anything else, absolutely none are essential.

You cannot purchase your way to lucidity.

As a lucid explorer you should travel light, relying primarily upon your wit and wiles.

You already possess all that you need. Everything else is optional.

A pen and a sturdy journal are amongst the most useful additions, and, occasionally, a book or two offering advice from fellow travellers may be of use.

However, there are no shortcuts and no set path.

Travel light.

Invest your time and energy, not your money.

DREAM

Return to this page within a dream.

It will tell you exactly what you need to know.

ANOMALY

The world of dreams operates under its own rules.

The mind is a force of nature and dreams are a strange and lonesome outcrop.

This is an ancient and whimsical space.

One must recognise the mannerisms of the mind, all its subtle quirks and glitches.

A lucid dreamer must learn to speak the language of dreams, to recognise its syntax.

The vocabulary of the mind evolved in an analogue world, and dreams reflect this predisposition.

Our dreams struggle to translate the devices of our digital world, and often one will find they malfunction within their realm.

These and other anomalies are common in dreams. Learn to notice them.

STARS

We are surrounded by a multitude of shimmering lights, each a doorway to another world.

We must ask ourselves, do we pay more attention to those of the electronic variety, the glimmering screens of our phones and computers, than the ancient stars that fill the night sky?

If we find it easier to name the stars of our media than the astronomical variety, then perhaps our priorities are somewhat skewed.

Since the dawn of humanity, the stars have been a nightly reminder of the mystery of existence.

Their presence is, perhaps, the ultimate antidote to the folly of human conceit, a reminder that we are small creatures adrift in a primordial riddle.

When we combine stargazing with knowledge, taking the time to learn the names, nature and secrets of the objects in the night sky, we not only become familiar with the cosmos but we build a more robust and complex inner world.

DELUSION

It is easy to fall for the allure of a comforting delusion.

In a universe that is vast and unpredictable, we can be forgiven for attempting to find solace in reassuring fables.

We humans are storytellers, and since the dawn of time, we have flown on the wings of imagination, soaring through myth and make-believe.

Even in dreams we become the authors of our own private fictions and, without lucidity, we blindly accept their reality.

Imagination has the power to move and inspire, but we must be wary of its propensity to cloud our judgement and our hunger to allow it to do so.

We must strive to avoid being fooled, knowing well that we are experts in fooling ourselves.

ENVIRONMENT

The space in which one lives is a reflection of the psyche. It is as a mirror reflecting itself.

Remember, we experience the world via a mental model and the space in which we live exists in tandem with our mental space.

Carefully consider the influence of your surroundings, be cognizant to the feedback loop between mind and environment.

A clean and organised environment lends itself to a lucid and disciplined mind.

MEDITATION

Meditation is often seen as a discrete activity, something one sets aside the time to perform.

We imagine sage individuals calmly adopting the lotus position and venturing within.

However, traditionally, the act of a sitting meditation was often used as a beginners aid, a starting point for those who were unable to establish the meditative mindset during daily pursuits.

Meditation is a state of mind that can be achieved during any undertaking.

While sitting meditation can be a useful tool for focus and development, the primary aim is to bring this mindset into the activities of daily life.

While it may seem glamorous to put aside quiet time for meditation, be wary that this can become a form of ostentation, a distraction from its practical applications.

Meditation is a tool, not a statement of identity.

MUNDANE

Those seeking a lucid life or undertaking a philosophical or spiritual path should be careful to avoid becoming detached from, or dismissive of, the physical world.

It is easy to become wrapped up in grand esoteric ideas, to drift into the egotistical and conceited notions that one is somehow above such concerns.

We are the product of the natural world, and we are little more than a young species of somewhat knowledgeable primates.

As such, it is important to remain grounded. We must remind ourselves that all the grandeur of our inner worlds depends entirely upon the foundations of physical processes.

Furthermore, the mundane glistens with beauty, pleasure and wonder.

The machinery of the physical world bursts with hidden secrets and knowledge.

BOREDOM

Boredom is a luxury.

It is a gift bestowed to us through the tribulations and toil of our ancestors.

The universe owes us nothing.
It is under no obligation to entertain or nurture us.

We have tamed our world and earnt valuable time.

It is our responsibility to spend it well.

DIVISION

Spend time studying the nature of division.
It is a valuable meditation.

Explore how the mind chooses to divide and separate the world.

Question the logic behind such choices—where light becomes dark, sleep becomes wakefulness, self becomes other.

Investigate how your choice of divisions differ from those of others, and learn to see the subjectivity behind this.

Notice the subtle gradients that exist between all things.

Is there division at all?

RITUAL

For all of its esoteric connotations, ritual is a practical and powerful tool.

It can instigate profound psychological change through focus, belief and repetition.

It is certainly no coincidence that ritual is deeply embedded in human culture, acting as a core principle for many of life's most meaningful events.

When approaching lucidity, be it in dreams or life, developing your own private rituals can transform your practice.

It can be as simple as taking the time to ponder lucidity each time you witness the moon, or, for the creative among you, an elaborate spiritual event.

Study the rituals of various cultures and devise your own based upon their common principles.

Remember, consistency and repetition are key.

MEMORY

Dreams are woven from the fabric of memory.

Each night, we venture among the dusty corridors of remembrance.

We flit like fireflies between abstractions, igniting fragments of the forgotten.

A lucid mind must learn to master memory.

We must dispel the fog of forgetting and build bridges in the mind.

Practise and hone your skill of recollection.

It is the master key to the door of dreaming.

FRAGMENTS

Who are those who walk among our dreams?
Those wayward fragments of self,
the scattered children of persona.

We are each a multitude, a buzzing hive of minds and selves.

Listen carefully to the voice of the Oneiroi, those players in the theatre of the night, for together they are the playwrights of the self.

We hide our secrets in the citizens of nocturnal cities, giving faces to our passions so they may live within us.

Learn from them.

ART

The ineffable,
Finds its life in dreams and art.
Seeding reflection.

FORAGE

The dreamscape is an environment ripe with inspiration.

One of the most expedient means of building a bridge between the dreaming and waking mind is to manifest the inventiveness of dreams in our daily lives.

Through this practice we add practical value to our dreams, strengthening our connection to them.

This can be achieved in any number of ways, from the use of dreams to inspire complicated creative works such as music or art, to more mundane matters, such as influencing our choice of attire, furnishings, or daily activities.

Become a forager of dreams. Hunt for ways in which your dreams can influence life.

REASON

One should apply reason, scepticism, and critical thinking to all aspects of the lucid adventure.

Such an approach is a core principle in the lifestyle of a lucid dreamer.

This is more than learning to be critical of the differences between dreaming and wakefulness.

We are encouraging lucid thought towards all areas of life. This is a far more effective and rewarding approach.

Not only shall you become more frequently lucid in your dreams but you'll be less easily misled by the delusions and fantasies that can manifest in all aspects of life.

VALIDITY

There are a few simple questions that one can use to assess the validity of a lucidity product or teacher:

- Has the person or product a traceable and established history in the field?
- Does the product appear to be jumping on a bandwagon such as a popular movie or unscientific concept?
- Do the claims that are being made sound too good to be true?
- Do any endorsements stem from a related group of professionals?
- Are the boundaries between established scientific fact, speculation and personal beliefs carelessly blurred?
- Does the person or company accept criticism of their work, or are their social feeds highly censored?

FRONTIER

Despite humanity's many scientific advances, there is still little consensus in the field of consciousness.

While we are making steady and continued progress, our understanding of the mind remains incomplete and lacks cohesion.

It is important to remember that our many theories are works in progress. At this point in history, it is wise to be suspicious of those who claim to have all the answers.

As it stands, we each stand before an untamed wilderness, which beckons those with a spirit for adventure.

The mind offers us the rare chance for true exploration.

We are each a pioneer of an ancient and untamed frontier.

PAREIDOLIA

The human mind has evolved as a powerful system for pattern recognition.
Embedded deep within our psyche is a deep craving for identification.

So strong is this drive that we are prone to imagine faces and animals in random visual noise—the shape of clouds, the texture of trees, and so forth.

This hungry instinctual form of hallucination is known as pareidolia.

We can use pareidolia as a doorway into the creative imagination.

Practice hunting pareidolic phenomena in the waking world, become familiar with their nature, and allow them to trigger the imagination.

Then, in the expectation-driven realm of dreams, one can allow pareidolia to flower, populating the dreamscape with entities born of pandemonium.

MOMENT

Attempt to capture the moment when waking becomes sleep.

Be aware at the shoreline between worlds, remaining firm in the spiralling waves of hypnagogic surf.

Succumb to sleep's currents without drowning in her darkness.

Hold fast to the raft of lucidity and drift with the tide of dreams.

EPOCH

In our dreams time is fluid.

Each night we traverse life's epochs, skimming effortlessly through time.

We may relive the haunts of our youth, or conjure facsimiles of history or strange and unknowable futures.

Our dreams appear to tear apart the fabric of physics and offer the power to manipulate time itself.

Yet it is a world of models and memories, an illusory temporal playground.

When we explore our relationship with time, we realise that everything beyond the eternal now is a mind playing with memories and predictions.

Lucidity can only ever exist in the present moment.

WHY

In our clamouring to attain lucidity, it is easy to forget our motivations.

It is important to regularly ask,
"Why do I want this?"

Without a firm understanding of the root of our ambitions, we can become untethered, drifting without direction.

Regularly investigate and define your goals. They are your foundations.

ARCHETYPE

Personality is a hairsbreadth film upon the deep and vast ocean of self.

Raging beneath identity is a feral world of instinct, archetype, and myth.

"I" floats like a paper boat upon this thellasic underworld, in a tenuous balance between its foundation and destruction.

"I" is the shimmering illusion of the rainbow. "Self", the raging storm at its foundation.

You are larger, deeper, wilder than "I".

INSOMNIA

Stirring the pond never stills its waters.
Sleep is a forgetting and cannot be forced.

Insomnia cannot be tackled directly.
Instead, when one cannot sleep, simply stop trying.

Prodding the hive of the mind will only enliven it.

Distract yourself and wait for sleep to call to you.

DIET

There is a common assumption that diet can have an important influence on dreams and the mind.

As a result, a large and thriving market has evolved selling supplements and other dietary aids.

The reality is that a healthy and balanced diet will generally supply all the nutritional requirements for a fully functional mind.

Supplementation is generally only effective when the body is deficient, and any effects will be seen in contrast to this, lasting only until balance is restored.

Supplements that have a noticeable impact on healthy individuals should be approached with caution. They should be considered pharmaceuticals.

As with any performance enhancing drug, gains generally come with side effects and hidden costs.

SIMULATION

You and everyone you'll ever know are intricately complex biological machines, organic computers designed to create astoundingly elaborate reality simulations.

The social, technological, linguistic and creative interactions between these sentient bio-simulations creates an ever expanding web of larger, more complex illusions.

Importantly, these simulations are far from perfect; they contain flaws and loopholes.

All too often we mistake the map for the territory and open ourselves to cognitive dissonance and error. We become lost in our own living dreams.

As with any complex network, even small errors can ripple outwards creating a snowball effect that, left unchecked, can cause system-wide issues.

We each program our world with our words and deeds. We must take this responsibility seriously.

FOOLISH

Be playful in your journey.

Do not be afraid to appear foolish and free.

In all the mystery and wonder of this world, there is a secret: the wiseman and the fool are indistinguishable.

Joy turns work into play.
Silliness is the soul of humility.
Laughter levels us all.

Embarrass yourself, take risks, play the fool.

Never take yourself too seriously.

You may find it is the least foolish way of all.

QUALIA

There is an essence to all things that is beyond expression.

We call these qualia.

We cannot know if our personal experience of qualia is unique, or if we all share this ineffable language.

It is the soul of matter, the animus of things.

We find it in the wordless aspects of a shadow or the "personality" of water.

In qualia lies riddles.
It calls into question the very relationship between consciousness and the material world.

Where and what is qualia?

SECURITY

It is in our nature to crave security.

We invest our days building fragile barriers from the chaos beyond.

Our species, in its endless creativity, has erected elaborate structures of world and mind.

In our folly we believe we can forever shield ourselves from the storm.

Yet, for all our cunning, we must exist in the wilderness of being.

Whatever our fortresses, we mustn't forget their fallibilities.

We must accept that true security is an illusion.

Lucidity lives in a wild heart.

FALSEHOODS

Lies move fast and smile sweetly.
They stir our senses, inflate our egos and console the inconsolable.

When one embarks upon an investigation into the mind, be it through dreaming, drugs, meditation or otherwise, one must be prepared to encounter the intoxicating allure of many falsehoods.

One would not dream of diamonds and expect to awaken wealthy.

So too, the glittering revelations of mind exploration can be equally as illusory.

One must be the most wary of those things which appeal or flatter.

DROUGHT

Focus is finite.

Though we may wish for infinite awareness, the mind is bound by the constraints of biology.

In our practices of lucidity, there will be times of drought, when all ability seems lost.

Consider this no more than the blisters of an overenthusiastic athlete.

When drought comes, do not be disheartened.
Pay attention to it.

It is a time to recuperate and reassess your approach.

HYPE

Few words are needed.

This reflects the reality of lucidity.

Dedication and observation are the tools.

Avoid those selling hype and hyperbole.
That is an infinite and empty well of tuition.

Study a thousand maps and one becomes a cartographer.

The only meaningful journey is the one embarked upon.

WHO

Who learns?

Who is aware?

Who becomes lucid?

PROGRAMMING

If you are anything like the vast majority of modern humans, you have almost certainly developed a habit of regularly becoming lost in technology.

You likely reach for your phone more often than necessary, looking for the next hit of information, or a distraction from tedium.

This form of habitual tendency is the antithesis of lucidity.

To counter this slow technological dulling of the senses, attempt to hijack this habit.

Each time you reach for your phone or become lost in technology, repay this debt by spending an equal or larger time invested in the now.

Explore the immediate world around you and invest your full attention into every detail. Interact, immerse, live.

Become aware of all your bad habits and attempt to do this for each of them.

LUCID

The man who climbs the mountain kills the mountain.

To him it is no longer the distant stranger, the beautiful view.

It is toil and rocks, ice and pain.

The summit's sweeping view is witnessed only by those with blistered hands and aching muscles.

Each journey requires a sacrifice,
the death of comfort and naivety.

Lucidity comes at a cost.

UNPLUG

Often in this hyper-connected world, we can feel as if we stand on a stage, with an audience of sixteen billion eyes, all staring, waiting to pass judgement.

We're social creatures, and after aeons of evolution, it is deeply embedded within our genetics to please the crowd—to win favour with the tribe.

However, we no longer live in the small communities of our ancestors, where competition was low, where standing out simply meant being the best among a few hundred individuals. We now live in a new world, where our tribe has expanded to encompass all of humanity. It's a place in which one's personal achievements stand toe to toe in a digital marketplace facing the very cream of our species. We believe ourselves to be competing against the world's most beautiful, talented, spiritual and knowledgeable.

We all crave recognition. It's a core element of the human condition. Yet how can one fill this need when we are bombarded by an endless digital feed of curated polished perfection from around the globe?

It comes as no surprise that diagnosis of depression is currently at an all time high, and that the politics of identity have become such an obsession amongst the young. How much easier it is to find meaning in the arbitrary accidents of our birth rather than face the seemingly insurmountable challenge of being noticed, of being "important", among a crowd so large we cannot even conceptually grasp the number.

Maybe we're using the wrong yardstick?

Eight billion and growing. This is the population of planet earth today. Can the human mind really conceive how vast this is? Yet each day, our social feeds, YouTube videos and our internet searches filter through the vast and diverse cosmos of humanity to hand-pick a pixel of a fraction of a mote, bringing us the "very best" of what humanity has to offer. It's then portrayed as if this is "normal"—as if this is what we are to expect of ourselves. What a very beautiful illusion and hideous expectation we have woven.

How convenient it is for those who wish to govern us, or for those wishing to sell products that will "improve life", that the bar has been set so very high. We all feel so far from what we are told is perfect that we'll readily accept the help of anyone who claims to offer a solution.

As this web grows tighter, we may fool ourselves into believing that planet earth is, indeed, very small. How very claustrophobic we can feel, how much more terrifying life becomes when the atrocities and horrors of the entire world bombard our ancient, provincial brains; when the opinions and acts of complete strangers are delivered to us as if they were letters from a loved one.

We are social creatures. We empathise, we edit ourselves to find acceptance among the tribe. Yet when the physical barriers of distance have become almost meaningless, with the global homogeneous hand-picked feed entering each of our minds, how quickly our individuality and cultures can shrink, as we all struggle to imitate the same role models, to mimic the best the world has to offer. We shrug off or ignore that which makes us unique in order to squeeze ourselves into an imaginary cookie cutter.

Our technology is a marvel and our species' ability to work together is astounding. We have solved so many of our oldest problems and we carry the world's finest knowledge, art, and wonders only a few clicks away in our pockets. Still, we must not forget that with each new solution, every new invention, comes a new set of challenges, new problems.

As the saying goes, 'You can't please all of the people all of the time', and how staggeringly true this really is when 'all of the people' refers to the entire population of our beautiful planet.

Sometimes it is worth taking a step back. To remind ourselves that our technology, as wonderful as it is, has created a dream in which we can so easily lose our lucidity.

It's important to remember that the world is far more vast

than it may seem, that beauty, talent, ideas, and wisdom are infinitely more varied than that which appears on our screens, that things still feel more meaningful when we directly touch the lives of those who are closest to us, when our actions fill and embrace all of our senses.

While we should continue to use our technology to help break down barriers and to work together to improve our world, we mustn't let ourselves lose sight of our reality.

As comfortable as the delusion may be, to believe that as an individual we are the exception, that we are somehow chosen, it's simply common sense to accept that this is almost certainly not the case.

We cannot all be the "golden monkey", the tiny fraction of humanity that achieves the very best and is noticed by all. Yes, we can strive for perfection, but perhaps we should decide for ourselves what we consider to be perfect. We certainly shouldn't chase a rainbow of another's devising at the cost of our sanity or our self-respect.

Sometimes it's good to remember that whatever your flaws, whatever your problems, however far you are from the global social concept of "perfection", you are a unique entity in the vastness of time and space. You are a fleeting but absolutely one-of-a-kind being, the result of an ancient universe playing with chaos.

So be kind to yourself, let your hair down, stop judging

yourself so harshly.

In a world built from nature juggling with imperfections, you are imperfectly perfect. Just be yourself, love yourself, and remember that you get to choose your own standards and to question all you are told. Unplug a little more often and connect with reality. Enjoy your meal without the urge to photograph it, have an adventure that nobody else knows about, revel in the freedom that privacy offers, embrace simplicity.

It needn't be some spiritual revelation. It's simply a case of being here and being you. Not caring what the global audience thinks, not needing to tweet and share. Unplugged, unjudged and free to play in the universe.

It's also good to remind oneself that in a cosmos as vast and old as ours, the entirety of humanity's achievements are as insignificant as that of an electron in a wild storm.

You and your problems are much smaller than you may believe.

It rarely matters what the world thinks of you, and anyhow, the world probably isn't paying attention, it's far too busy worrying what everyone else thinks of it.

So relax, set your own standards, ignore those who make you feel worthless, and strive to be the best you can here and now.

Rediscover the real value and meaning of the words 'share', 'like' and 'friends'. Embrace the joy of simplicity.

In other words, the reality that matters exists beyond the little black techno-frames of our world and is waiting for you to embrace it.

Be yourself.

ACKNOWLEDGMENTS

This book exists due to the kind support of many wonderful individuals.

For their creativity, friendship, patience, and practical input, I thank Madeleine Hopkins and Samuel Davidson.

For their support, kindness, and patronage, my warmest thanks go to:

Nyx, Andrew Brown, Anka Sterling, Al Wadlan, Marlise Brauchli, Janie Smallridge, Uwe Krüger, Patrick Raithofer, Rhett McLaughlin, James Anderson, Mismagius, Jeffery Mcveigh, Dylan Rispoli, Jeremy Kear, Daniel, Ferenc Molnar, and Stephen Duniven.

I consider you all dear friends and wish you a lifetime of adventure and discovery.

FIN